Skyscrapers

Maria Koran and John Willis

EYEDISCOVER

Go to **www.eyediscover.com** and enter this book's unique code.

BOOK CODE

AVG32968

EYEDISCOVER brings you optic readalongs that support active learning.

Published by AV2
276 5th Avenue, Suite 704 #917
New York, NY 10001
Website: www.eyediscover.com

Library of Congress Control Number: 2021937119

ISBN 978-1-7911-4012-0 (hardcover)

Printed in Guangzhou, China
1 2 3 4 5 6 7 8 9 0 25 24 23 22 21

042021
102120

Project Coordinator: John Willis
Designer: Mandy Christiansen

The publisher acknowledges Getty Images, Alamy, and Shutterstock as the primary image suppliers for this title.

EYEDISCOVER provides enriched content, optimized for tablet use, that supplements and complements this book. EYEDISCOVER books strive to create inspired learning and engage young minds in a total learning experience.

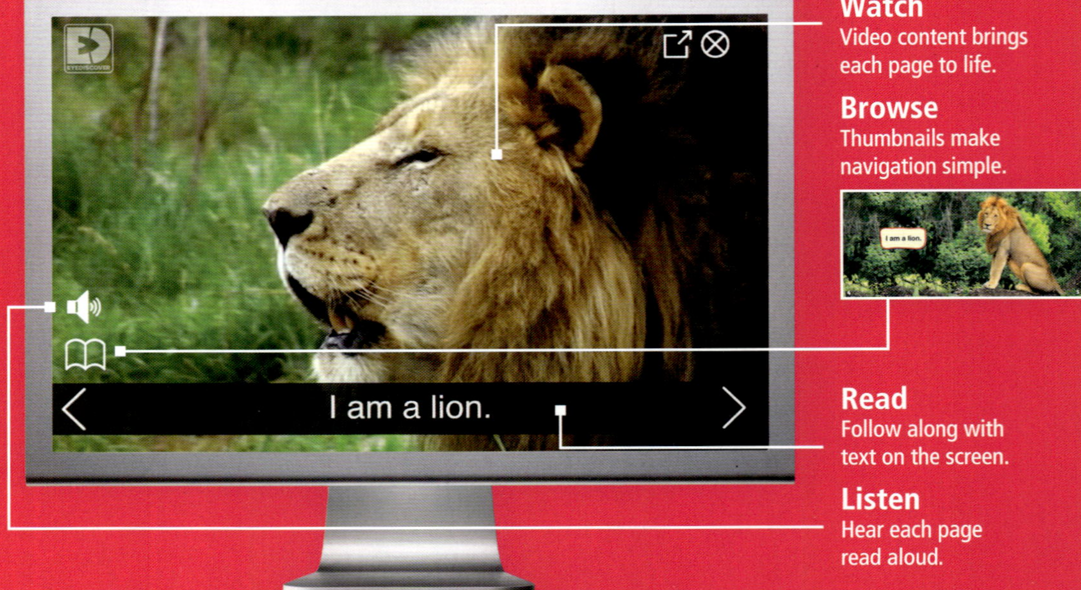

Your EYEDISCOVER Optic Readalongs come alive with...

Audio
Listen to the entire book read aloud.

Video
High resolution videos turn each spread into an optic readalong.

OPTIMIZED FOR
- TABLETS
- WHITEBOARDS
- COMPUTERS
- AND MUCH MORE!

This title is part of our EyeDiscover digital subscription

1-Year EyeDiscover Subscription
ISBN 978-1-4896-8346-5

Access all EyeDiscover titles with our digital subscription.
Sign up for a FREE trial at **www.eyediscover.com/trial**

Skyscrapers

In this book, you will learn about

- what they are
- what they look like
- where they are

and much more!

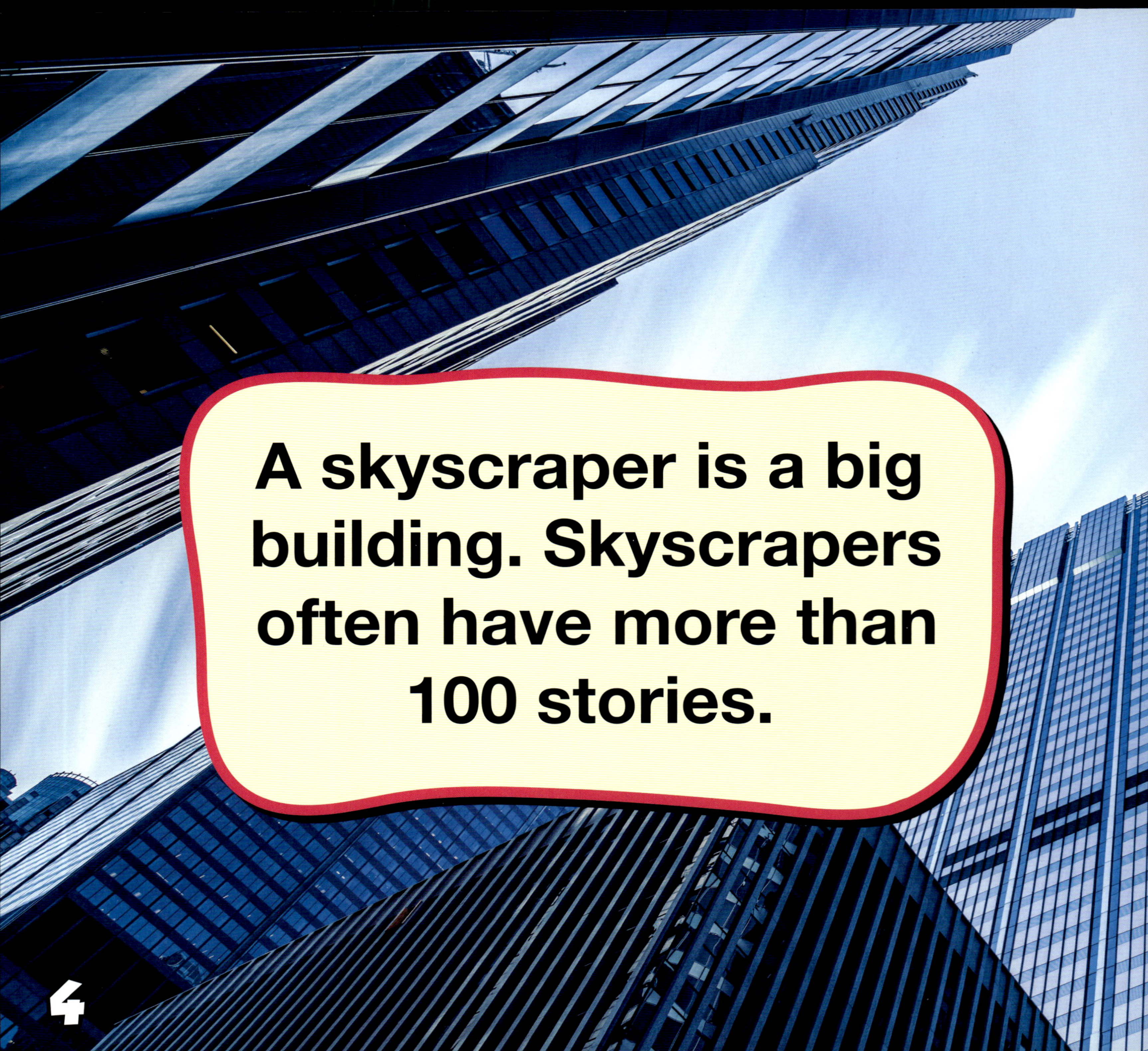

A skyscraper is a big building. Skyscrapers often have more than 100 stories.

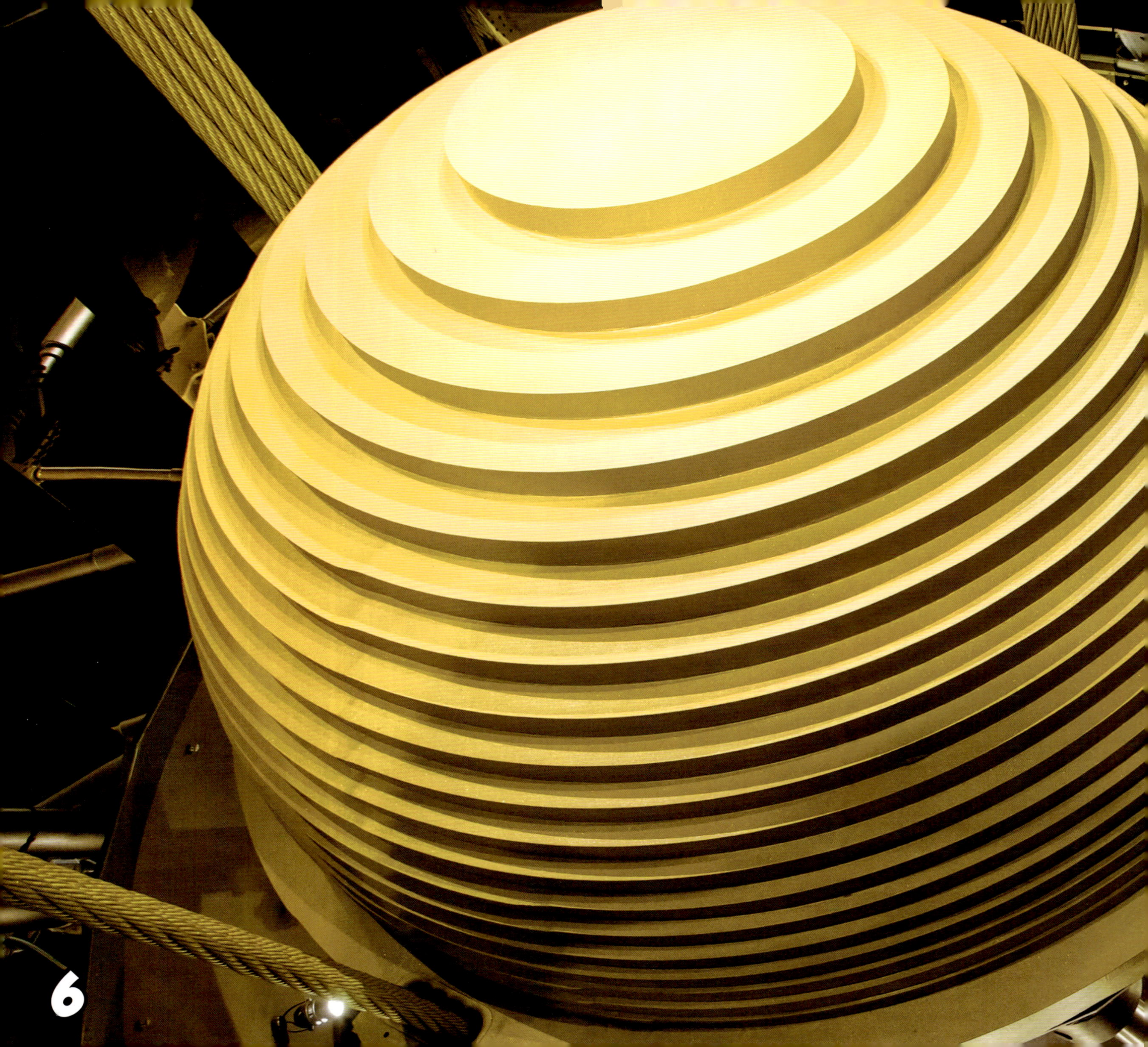

Skyscrapers move or sway in the wind. Some use heavy weights to keep steady.

Many skyscrapers have special decks. People can visit them to see things from high up.

One early American skyscraper is the Flatiron Building in New York City.

W 23 St
Westbound
KEEP RIGHT
ONE WAY
MAD.
SQ.
ART.
at&t

One very tall skyscraper is Taipei 101. It was the world's tallest building until 2010.

The tallest skyscraper in North America is called the One World Trade Center.

The Petronas Towers are in the country of Malaysia. They were the tallest buildings in the world for six years.

Another very tall skyscraper is the Shanghai Tower in China. Only one building is taller.

中国太平
CHINA TAIPING

The Burj Khalifa is the tallest building in the world. It is more than half a mile tall.

The word "skyscraper" was **first used** about **140 years** ago.

Taipei 101 was the **first building** to be more than **1,640 FEET** (500 meters) **tall**.

The **Burj Khalifa** took **6 years** to build.

Each of the **PETRONAS TOWERS** has **88** stories.

The **Shanghai Tower's elevators** can move at speeds of **46 miles** (74 kilometers) **per hour**.

The **Flatiron Building** was built in **1902**.

KEY WORDS

Research has shown that as much as 65 percent of all written material published in English is made up of 300 words. These 300 words cannot be taught using pictures or learned by sounding them out. They must be recognized by sight. This book contains 43 common sight words to help young readers improve their reading fluency and comprehension. This book also teaches young readers several important content words, such as proper nouns. These words are paired with pictures to aid in learning and improve understanding.

Page	Sight Words First Appearance
4	a, big, have, is, more, often, than
7	in, keep, move, or, some, the, to, use
8	can, from, high, many, people, see, them, things, up
10	American, city, new, one
13	it, until, very, was, world
17	are, country, for, of, they, were, years
18	another, only
20	mile

Page	Content Words First Appearance
4	building, skyscraper, stories
7	weights, wind
8	decks
10	Flatiron Building, New York City
13	Taipei 101
14	North America, One World Trade Center
17	Malaysia, Petronas Towers
18	China, Shanghai Tower
20	Burj Khalifa

Watch
Video content brings each page to life.

Browse
Thumbnails make navigation simple.

Read
Follow along with text on the screen.

Listen
Hear each page read aloud.

Go to www.eyediscover.com and enter this book's unique code.

BOOK CODE

AVG32968